BOB GELDOF

by Charlotte Gray

Picture Credits

Associated Press — 38, 39 (below), 40, 42, 43, 45 (left); © David Bailey (from *Imagine, a book for Band Aid*) — 27 (top); Lafayette, Dublin — 4, 6, 8; London Features International Ltd. — Steve Rapport 39 (top), 44 (below left): Ken Regan, Camera 5, 48-9; Marconi Space Systems — 33; © Tony McGrath —19, Duncan Paul Associates — Brian Aris 34; the Press Association Ltd. — 23, 54, 58; Retna Pictures Ltd. — Adrian Boot 13, 41, 45 (right), 49 (below right), 60-1: Larry Buscacca 44 (top): Mike Kegan 16: Paul Slattery 17; *Sunday Times* London from *With Geldof in Africa* — Frank Herrmann 21, 24, 27 (below), 52-3, 56, 57; Times Books Ltd. from *With Geldof in Africa* — 25; Universal Pictorial Press & Agency Ltd. — 36-7.
Map on page 11 drawn by Geoffrey Pleasance.
   Our grateful thanks go to the many agencies and photographers for their help and especially to David Bailey, Tony McGrath and Times Books Ltd. for donating their fees directly to Band Aid.

To Emily

North American edition first published in 1988 by
Gareth Stevens, Inc.
7317 W. Green Tree Road
Milwaukee, WI 53223 USA

Library of Congress Cataloging-in-Publication Data

Gray, Charlotte, 1928-
     Bob Geldof: the pop star who raised $140 million for famine relief in Ethiopia.
     (People who have helped the world)
     Includes index.
     Summary: Follows the early years, musical career, and charity work of the musician who organized the Live Aid project and raised more money for the starving in Africa than anyone else in the world.
     1. Geldof, Bob, 1954- — Juvenile literature. 2. Rock musicians — Ireland — Biography — Juvenile literature. [1. Geldof, Bob, 1954- \ 2. Musicians. 3. Live Aid (Fund raising enterprise)] I. Title. II. Series
ML3930.G27G7 1988   784.5'4'00924 [B]   88-2231
ISBN 1-55532-814-8 (lib. bdg.)
ISBN 1-55532-839-3

C   921
     GEL

Series conceived and edited by Helen Exley.
Picture research: Diana Briscoe.
Research assistant: Margaret Montgomery.
Series editor, U.S.: Rhoda Irene Sherwood.
Editorial assistant, U.S.: Mary Thomas
Additional end matter, U.S.: Ric Hawthorne.

Printed in Hungary

1 2 3 4 5 6 7 8 9 93 92 91 90 89 88

BOB GELDOF

*The rock star who raised $140 million
for famine relief in Ethiopia*

by Charlotte Gray

Gareth Stevens Publishing
Milwaukee

4

Early days

Robert Frederick Zenon Geldof was born in Ireland in 1954, on the edge of Dublin, that beautiful, down-at-heel, talkative city. His father's parents had come from Ypres, in Belgium, in 1914 to escape from the First World War, while his mother's parents were German. His unusual middle name was chosen by his father. Bob said on television, "I was named after an inert gas. My father wanted to call me Zeus Zenon, but my mother wouldn't wear it!"

He has two sisters, who are much older than he. Their names are Cleo and Lynn. Geldof told *Melody Maker* in 1979, "It's a really strong family. Like, kissing and hugging all the time."

As a very small boy, with loving parents, two older sisters, and his extra-special Auntie Fifi, Bob had plenty of room to play and plenty of good times. He was busy and happy and bright.

Just before he was due to start school, the family moved to a big, gloomy house in Dun Laoghaire, three miles from Dublin. His dad brightened it with new paint, and the cheerful life seemed set to go on as before. Then overnight everything changed. His pretty, funny mother died very suddenly, so suddenly that, at the age of seven, Bob could scarcely understand what had happened. Cleo took over the running of the household, though she was only sixteen, because their dad was a salesman and away all week. Lynn was still at school, like Bob.

About five years later, Cleo became very ill with leukemia. She was expected to die within six months when she was taken on a pilgrimage to Lourdes in southern France. What happened there nobody knows, but she returned completely cured. Shortly afterwards, she got married and moved away to her

Opposite: Bob Geldof at school at Blackrock College, Dublin. This photo shows Bob looking neat and happy. But like some teenagers, Bob grew more untidy, more rebellious. His teachers might have guessed that he would grow up to be a famous rock star. But no one would have guessed that he would mastermind the biggest concert in the world nor that he would also raise, with the help of many supporters, more money for the starving in Africa than any other person in the world.

5

On days when school was just too much like prison, Bob would get away from it all and spend his lunchtime sitting on the sea wall, looking out into the bay.

own home. Lynn had also left, so Bob was alone in that big house that seemed very gloomy to a small boy on his own.

To make things worse, because his father was away so much and there was no one at home until the late evening, Bob was sent as a day pupil to Blackrock College, an expensive Catholic private school. He had to stay there for his evening meal and for the evening study period. His friends all went off to their homes and families at the usual time, leaving Bob behind in the company of the boarders. He had to eat at a table on his own, and the boarders mocked him because he was only a day boy. The staff of the school saw what was happening. They tried to be kind, but it was a very old-fashioned sort of school, strict and unimaginative. Bob hated it, and although he was much liked by some of his teachers, he was never really happy.

Although intelligent, Bob never did very well at school. On more than one occasion, he misled his father as to his grades. Of course, his father was even angrier when he found out the truth.

Bob already showed signs of enjoying performing before an audience. Pupils were sometimes asked to perform something before supper. Unlike his fellow students who dreaded being asked to perform, Bob often volunteered. On one occasion in 1961, he sang the latest hit, "The Clancy Brothers and the Holy Grail," for his supper.

Bob was getting older — awkward and scruffy, but intelligent and restless. As far as the school was concerned, he was difficult indeed.

When he was fourteen, all Bob seemed to be interested in was clothes and rock groups like The Rolling Stones, The Who, and Small Faces. His father became more and more irritated by his untidiness and lack of enthusiasm.

Like other people his age, Bob wanted his own life to be quite different from his father's. He wanted to shake up his teachers, who he thought had set ideas that they would not allow to be questioned. He wanted to listen to music that older people did not seem to understand, music that was *his* music. The Rolling Stones spoke his language, and Mick Jagger made him feel less ugly and odd.

Bob's sister Cleo recently told London's *Today* newspaper that even at fourteen, Bob was an idealist. He was reading Sartre and not comics. "I think we learned a good deal from Daddy," said Cleo. "He always kept our minds working, made us aware of the world, taught us to question. But more than that he's a very kind man, always quietly helping people in trouble. So it wasn't off the wind Robert got it."

However hard things were at school and home, Bob had an honesty of outlook and a hatred of sham that has stayed with him until today. It has made him seem very arrogant and loudmouthed at times, and he has annoyed a lot of people. But it is not a question of conceit or showing off. He thinks hard before he speaks, makes sure of his facts, and says what he does because he believes passionately that something must be done. He still hates stupidity and bigotry and prejudice as he did then. He is against any kind of discrimination that encourages one group of people to consider themselves superior to another group, and so to deny them their right to a good and decent life. If he sometimes tips over the edge into downright

Blackrock College, the private school just outside Dublin, capital of Ireland. Bob Geldof hated every minute he was there.

rudeness, he feels that that is a more honest reaction than the bland, courteous lies that he thinks are used by many people in power.

His bad manners and cursing still earn Bob friends as well as enemies. In 1985, when Bob was touring Africa to help decide how the millions donated to charity would be spent, a *Sunday Times* newspaper correspondent reported that one aid worker had put it this way: "I disliked Geldof at first. I resented his arrogance, his punk style. Then he began talking sense, and if he can bully the agencies into working together, it will be a big success."

Bob still actually looks as scruffy as he was at school, but by now even heads of countries see that his beliefs and basic character are more important than his appearance.

Not all his teachers thought so. Life in his last years at school continued to be as bad as before — or worse. He was sometimes beaten over what seemed to him to be trivial matters. No one realized that this was making him behave even worse.

During his last year in school, he began working with one of the Simon Communities in Dublin. These were set up to help alcoholics, drug addicts, homeless down-and-outs, and people with mental illnesses. They provide basic shelter, food, clothing and medical care for anyone who arrives and is in need. Working in one of these houses must have been an eye opener for someone who came from a middle-class background.

Here were real people with real needs, instead of printed words, protest marches, and endless argument. Bob began to be able to see life through their eyes; problems were real, not abstract theory. Much later, this gift would help him to understand what it was like to live and die in the sun-shrivelled world of Africa.

He would spend two nights every week helping out at the Simon Community, getting to bed at five in the morning but still managing to get to school the next day. This was the real part of his life.

His academic work was no better than before. When he took his final exams, he simply put his name at the top of some of the exam papers and sat thinking of something else until the bell rang.

Despite his father's hopes that he would get *some* training, Bob had had enough. The moment school was over, he left for England.

FREE. More or less

Freedom from school meant the canning factory. Bob and his friends had been to England in the summer to make some money working the night shift in a factory that produced canned peas. It was a sickening, monotonous job. Whatever they did, they could not get rid of the nauseating smells or the stains on their skin from the green dye.

Once more in Ireland, he tried one job after another, but in the end he left for Britain again and landed a job with other Irishmen as a road construction worker. It taught him a lot about living, for they were a wild lot, the Irish road builders. But after a while he began to find that it wasn't for him, despite the jokes and the big money.

He drifted back and started living in various empty houses around London.

The next few months were aimless. Bob moved

from job to job, room to room. During this period he started smoking "pot" on a regular basis. But he had a bad trip that put him off all drugs for life. He now uses his fame actively to campaign against even the mildest drugs.

His living conditions and the drugs had left him sick and drifting, but he was determined to get well again. A friend of his, Shaun Finnigan, had been offered a job teaching English in a language school in Spain. Bob decided to go with him, but they had no money. Shaun recalled on the television show "This is Your Life" that they tried to scrape some money together by playing music on the streets outside the Odeon theater in the heart of London's Theatreland. "We only managed to make enough to get back to Brighton!" Eventually they made it to Spain and taught English. But after only a year the school closed down and Bob found himself back in Dublin. The walls seemed to close in on him. He felt aimless and depressed.

He began to plan his escape. This time he would try even farther afield — Canada. The money had to be raised from somewhere, and being Bob Geldof, he did not sit around looking for a job he fancied. He got work in a slaughter house. It was horrible. But he got the money to get out of Ireland.

It was in Canada that he began to find his feet. With only a little money in his pocket, living had to be done on a shoestring. Some of the boarding houses he was forced to stay in were downright appalling in their squalor and filthiness, but it was an adventure and it was all new to him.

As always, he was prepared to take any job at all to keep afloat, and this time he found himself working for a newspaper, the *Georgia Straight*, the third biggest-selling newspaper in Vancouver. He got a job on it as a music journalist. He told *Melody Maker* in 1979, "I said, in fact, that I'd been a *Melody Maker* writer when I got there!"

At first Bob kept things together by playing the role of a professional journalist. He later told a story on television about how he managed to persuade a

EIRE AND THE UNITED KINGDOM OF GREAT BRITAIN

Dublin
Dun Laoghaire
SCOTLAND
NORTHERN IRELAND
Liverpool
Lincoln
EIRE
ENGLAND
WALES
Cardiff
London
Davington

visiting pop group to hold a press conference for the paper. He had to park his dirty green Volkswagen some distance from the hotel so it would not be seen. Bob arrived with an impressive array of photographic and recording equipment. Although he may have looked the part, in fact neither camera nor tape recorder were loaded because he could not afford any film or tape! As usual, Bob got the job done.

But soon Bob found that he could write, that he loved writing, and that he could make a good living from it. He was made music editor and covered the pop scene right across the country. His opinions were sought after and his friendship, too.

When he had become a famous rock star, Bob was

Bob is Irish and was born in the capital of Eire, Dublin. When he was still a child, the Geldof family moved to Dun Laoghaire, just fifty-seven miles by ferry from England. Today Bob lives in London and he has a second home in Davington, Kent.

to tour the States and talk about this period to a newspaper: "I got into journalism and I started getting my name in the paper and then I became a minor personality in Vancouver. I appeared there on TV, you know. And I enjoyed it a lot and I wanted more of it. For the first time in my life, I was being recognized as an individual who had some thoughts and could put them on paper and be respected and recognized for them."

At long last Bob Geldof felt alive and confident, brimming with ideas and energy. He wanted to stay in Canada forever.

He had been there for three years, but to immigrate he had to get the proper documents, which meant going back to Ireland during 1975 to complete the paperwork.

Back in Dublin, he lost some of his newfound enthusiasm for life. While he waited to go back to Canada, he decided to start a free newspaper, like the ones that were proving to be so successful in Vancouver. It proved to be far more difficult than it would have been in progressive Canada, but he had made a beginning.

Getting nowhere

In the meantime, some of Bob's old friends had formed a shambling rock group that rehearsed in the living room of one of their parents' houses. The original members were Pete Briquette, Gerry Cott, Simon Crowe, Johnnie Fingers and Gary Roberts. All but Simon lived in Dun Laoghaire and had experimented with music without being committed to it. As bass player Pete Briquette said in 1979 to a reporter from *Melody Maker*, "I wasn't interested in joining any bands, but when we heard Dr. Feelgood, we thought we would have a go. I mean, I never went to any gigs in Dublin at all. None of us did. None of us were known at all. Before we started none of us had anything to do with that clique, that closed-shop kind of thing."

It was not until Bob returned that the group began to take off. According to Johnnie Fingers, who

played keyboards, Bob originally played the tambourine with them, but "His timing was so bad, we made him the lead singer." Gary, who played rhythm guitar, later suggested that Bob should be their manager and organize things for them.

Bob recalled later that he told the members of the group, "I didn't want the Boomtown Rats to be just another local band playing the Top 20 and earning a few quid each week. We had a timetable for success. I told them that if I joined we'd have to take it . . . seriously and really do something new and exciting. I knew that to succeed we'd have to choose a style and stick to it, to create an identity so that people would recognize us immediately."

Then, one day in September 1975, Gerry calmly announced that he'd got them a gig for Halloween. Only a month away. Bob's first thought was to wriggle out of it.

He asked how much they'd be getting. When Gerry told him $65.00, Bob said there was no way

Bob, Johnny, Pete, Gerry, Gary and Simon — alias the Boomtown Rats. They were one of the 1970s punk rock bands. Their early fame was a result not only of fierce lyrics and a hard primal beat but also of their co-stars — five live rats! Their first Number One single was "Rat Trap."

13

they would do it for that. He told the promoter they wouldn't do it for less than $135.00. Bob was certain he wouldn't agree.

The promoter accepted the deal without batting an eyelash. Now they *had* to do it!

The Boomtown Rats

Things were getting serious, and they were all wondering what they had let themselves in for. They didn't even have a name. Nightlife Thugs sounded good. Defiant. Outrageous.

In rising panic, they turned up at the hall on Halloween, pulled themselves together, went out onto the stage and began to play. In sheer disbelief, they watched the people dancing. The dancers seemed to enjoy their music, to believe they were a professional group. At the end there was a roar of applause. They felt like a real band!

During a break, an idea that was at the back of Bob's mind surfaced. He remembered a book he'd read about a teen gang in a boom town in the Oklahoma oilfields. Bob spoke to the promoter who wiped Nightlife Thugs from the blackboard and scrawled up, The Boomtown Rats.

At that time other bands didn't bother much with publicity or image. Bob saw things differently. If they were going to be a band, everyone should know about them. He had worked for the press; he knew about public relations. The band began to be noticed and featured in gossip columns of national newspapers. Fans started to ask for their autographs. It seemed incredible.

Bob became the spokesman for the band, but, decisions were made democratically. As Simon Crowe, the drummer, said, "Each member of the band contributes equally to the arrangement and development of the songs, although the original source of the material is usually Geldof. Bob is a good spokesman for the band. He knows how to handle it."

The Boomtown Rats succeeded because of their distinctive beat, their lively gigs, and their musical

talents. But Bob also added memorable publicity ideas. The outrageous gimmicks, such as awarding a pound of raw liver to the best dancer and projecting blue movies at the back of the stage during their gigs, delighted the Irish fans. The authorities were less amused, and soon the gigs were raided by the police on a regular basis. As Bob told *Melody Maker* in 1977, "Believe me, you just do not show blue movies in Ireland." However, their fame spread rapidly, and concerts were regularly sold out over two weeks in advance. On tour, they were often controversial. *The History of Rock* still records that a homecoming gig at Dublin's Leopardstown racetrack was banned by the local authorities who feared "riots and public insurrection."

With success, all Bob's old fears vanished. He had been good as a writer, but performing, he knew, was what he wanted to do more than anything in the world. Suddenly he was having fun.

Not that they were making enough money to live on. Bob, the rising pop idol, could be found delivering bread three days a week and, for the rest, doing door-to-door sales. Things were moving. Backed by even more outrageous publicity, they got more and more gigs. They were being reported in the music papers. The whole thing was spiralling faster than they could ever have believed.

They went on tour. Sometimes it was chaos, but their reward was playing at Dublin's National Stadium. They were a success, even if the expenses of the tour had left them each with only enough money for a new pair of shoes.

In April 1977, they set out for England with a tape and played a series of pubs and clubs around the country. The record companies soon heard about them, and six executives followed them to Ireland to try to put them on contract. Eventually they signed with Ensign Records, then a new company, because they liked its representative, Nigel Grainge, and admired his style.

Harry Doherty, who reviewed a concert of theirs soon after the contract was signed in 1977, noted that

Bob was "one of the few creatures of the New Wave who actually knows what he's talking about." He felt they had deliberately made their act theatrical, which put them way above any other New Wave band because it was based on audience communication. Bob talked to his audience instead of throwing the songs at them.

Another point was that they were opposed to the use of politically loaded lyrics in their songs, unlike many other New Wave groups. Bob told one reporter, "The crucial point is I genuinely don't want to feel that I've got anything to preach or that the band has anything to teach. We're not presumptuous enough to dare to tell people how to run their lives. I don't want kids to come to a political rally when they come to the Rats."

Fame and success

Suddenly the Boomtown Rats were far bigger than they had ever expected to be. By 1977, they moved to Britain, made their first hit single, "Looking After Number One," toured the North of England, did a television show in Ireland. Then "Top of the Pops" on BBC television. Then another album, *Tonic for the Troops*.

About this time, Paula Yates turned up. Bob, totally elated by the excitement of success, did not want to be tied down to any one girlfriend, but Paula had made up her mind. Wherever the band went, Paula went. In the end, Bob found he was in love with this persistent female, and they have been together ever since.

The success of the band took them everywhere — to America, Finland, Germany. By 1979, they had become the top band in Britain. Bob was under great pressure — writing songs, producing videos, doing interviews, creating ideas for artwork, performing every night.

Bob liked fame — it gave him the chance to speak out. And he did, sometimes shocking a good many people in the process.

Paula Yates was only seventeen when she met Bob. In the early days of his Boomtown Rats success, he did not want to become involved with her. But Paula won Bob over with a lethal combination of beauty and brains. Nine years later, they would marry. Paula herself would host the television show "The Tube" and would support Bob during his Band Aid and Live Aid work.

Success at that pitch could not last. Show business is a hard taskmaster, especially in the world of rock music. The public can turn against a band or an individual performer almost overnight.

After three years of success, the time came when the Boomtown Rats had not had a real hit for six months or more. The euphoria had burned itself out. In June 1982, Paula and Bob had just had their daughter, Fifi Trixiebelle, so it was the wrong time to have such serious money worries and an uncertain future. Only a short time before, the band had been on top of the world, but now, as happens so often to top stars, there was nothing but debts and anxiety. Their fifth and sixth albums — *Five Deep* (1982) and *In the Long Grass* (1984) — were liked by music critics but sold badly.

Bob would later describe this depressing period to *The Sun* newspaper: "One minute we were having a string of hits, the next minute we were yesterday's men. Our last four singles were played just fifteen times each on all radio stations. We were so broke that I remember waiting for the exchange rate to fluctuate so I could convert a check for a measly $400.00 to pay some bills.

"It was one of the most awful, soul-destroying periods of my life. We had to beg, borrow and steal to make a video."

Bob made the rounds over the next few months, trying to pick up the pieces, but nothing seemed to work out. One evening in October 1984, in a mood of black depression, he came home, flopped into a chair, and turned on the television.

What he saw made his troubles seem insignificant. What he saw changed his whole way of life and the lives of millions.

Band Aid

What Bob Geldof saw on television that night was famine. He saw people so shrunken by hunger that they were reduced to skin and bone — living skeletons, with their huge, hopeless eyes staring from their skull-like heads. A mother held her dying child,

too weak to cry or beg for help. A father held out a tightly wrapped bundle to be counted, the body of his little child. The reporter could scarcely speak at times because of anger and grief that this terrible thing had been allowed to happen.

It would have been shocking even if it had been one or two families reduced to such misery, but it was *tens of thousands of people*, starving to death before the eyes of the cameras — before *our* eyes.

Some European and American aid workers were there, but so little food had got through that they were having to pick out a handful of people still fit enough to stand a chance of survival. They gave what food there was to them. Those condemned to die watched them eat, apparently resigned to their own starvation. A truck appeared, crossing the dead and dusty plain, and those who could still run, ran — in the hope that there might be something, anything, to eat. One man ran far behind the others, burdened by the child he

In October 1984, the first horrible famine pictures were shown on television all over the world. The United Nations called it, "The greatest natural disaster faced by man."

19

Opposite: After Bob had seen starving children like this, he wasn't afraid to push and badger people. He would say anything and simply wear people down until they had to agree to help. Bob said later, "Maybe I was given my arrogance to do this." The prize was Britain's best-selling record of all time, and, most important of all, $10 million to save people in Ethiopia from death by starvation.

had on his back. He could not hope to get there in time, but he did not abandon his load.

Bob and all those millions sitting in their comfortable living rooms in the world's wealthy countries, with food and drink only a few steps away, stared at their television sets, stunned by what they were seeing.

He could not sleep that night. He kept seeing that man, like a bundle of dried sticks, running, running. The dying child in its mother's arms. The tiny shrivelled babies, with their huge, blank eyes.

What could he do? Send money, yes. But what else could he do?

Bob Geldof had neither the power of a politician nor the money of a millionaire. He was a pop musician. What could a pop musician do?

He could make a record and send the profits to Ethiopia. But the Boomtown Rats were going through rough times and were right out of the pop charts. Perhaps a record by them would not make enough money to be of any real use. He had completely forgotten his own money worries now. He was determined to do something to help these people. For them, what we call poverty would be untold wealth.

What about a record by the stars?

Then Bob had an idea. If a Boomtown Rats record wouldn't sell, maybe one made by top stars, big names, would. Midge Ure of Ultravox was a good friend. He phoned him, and Midge agreed at once.

He wanted to know if Bob already had a song. Bob had only half a song, half an idea, but nothing definite. Midge stepped in to help on the song. They decided on a name for their campaign to raise money through rock bands — Band Aid.

Bob phoned Sting and explained that he wanted to get out a record before Christmas to raise money for Ethiopia. Could he help?

Yes, he'd be there.

Bob was stunned. These were big names, famous people, constantly in demand, but they were only too

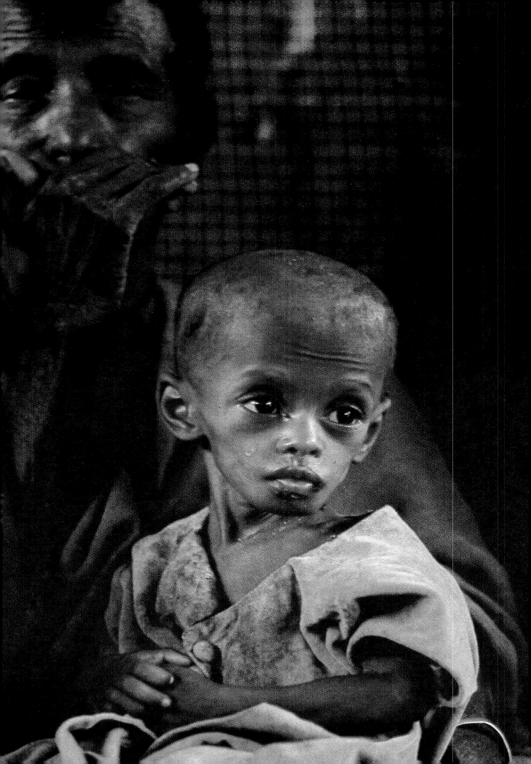

glad to help. Perhaps it was because he was one of them, a guy from another band.

Simon le Bon of Duran Duran: Yes, they'd be there too.

He bumped into Gary Kemp of Spandau Ballet. They were just off to Japan for a two-week tour but would be there if Bob could delay the recording.

That was going to be the problem. These people were in huge demand, booked up for months ahead. How could they all get together on one day to make the record?

But things did begin to fall into place. And to expand. It wasn't going to be just another record. It was going to be a massive effort, and it needed more and more names.

In the back of a taxi, Bob scribbled the words of a song on a page of his notebook. It seemed to write itself: "Do They Know It's Christmas?"

Bob was now caught up in the excitement. He phoned Boy George, Frankie Goes to Hollywood, Style Council, Human League. People were being so generous. The record company, manufacturers, printers, artists, and packers all gave their services free. But it was getting so big he had to face up to the need for real organization.

It could be big

Bowie and McCartney couldn't make it but would send recordings. The artwork came through. It was excellent. A date had to be chosen. Bob chose at random — Sunday, November 25, 1984.

A newspaper refused to give the record front-page coverage. That morning their front page had been filled by a picture of the back of the Princess of Wales' head. Bob exploded! How could they use the back of someone's head when this record would raise money for *millions* starving to death? He phoned the owner of the newspaper and he got his front page.

He'd learned a lesson. Always go right to the top.

Phil Collins, Paul Weller, Sting, and John Taylor from Duran Duran. The names poured in. He was working at top speed, all hours of the day and night.

The organization needed was incredible. He had never realized when he'd had the idea just what was going to be involved.

On Sunday, November 25, he half wondered whether anyone would turn up. He went down to the studio. Slowly, they began to drift in. Everyone. All the stars of the British pop industry. All, except Boy George. He was still in America.

Bob phoned him in New York.

Boy George caught the next Concorde and was there in time.

They finished mixing the record at seven the next morning. Immediately Bob took it to the British Broadcasting Company (BBC) and asked them to play it. All the time.

The BBC let him introduce it. He told listeners who was on the record, and what it was for. He told everyone to buy it for Christmas gifts, whether they liked pop music or not. Every record would mean lives saved.

Now he wanted it on "Top of the Pops." BBC television held back the show by five minutes so that "Do They Know It's Christmas?" could have the vital space between the news and the show. Britain's Number One that week was Jim Diamond, with his first hit record. When he was interviewed, he said, "I am delighted to be Number One, but next week I don't want people to buy my record, I want them to buy Band Aid instead."

Bob was amazed! The man had torpedoed his hit, his first, to help Ethiopia.

They were cutting 320 thousand copies of the record every day but they still couldn't cope with the increasing demand.

In the States it was outselling the top record by four hundred percent. In the first two weeks, a million-and-a-half copies had been sold.

Back in Britain, the Band Aid team sang "Do They Know It's Christmas?" on "Top of the Pops," just before the Queen's Christmas Day speech.

The idea of making a record to help Africa had succeeded beyond Bob's wildest hopes. By January 1985, the record had raised over $6.5 million.

Bob Geldof and Midge Ure receive the Ivor Novello Award for writing the Band Aid record "Do They Know It's Christmas?"

Ordinary people had found a way to help those starving millions. In spite of that, some cynics said it had just been a gimmick to boost Bob's career. The national press didn't think so. They urged him to go on, to go to Africa and see for himself. This was not what he had intended. It seemed too big, and he didn't want it all to be reduced to a newspaper story.

In the end he said he'd go, but only if there were no pictures of him with starving children, no tear-jerking publicity. On January 6, 1985, he flew to Addis Ababa, the capital of Ethiopia.

Ethiopia

Almost as soon as he landed, Bob began to see that

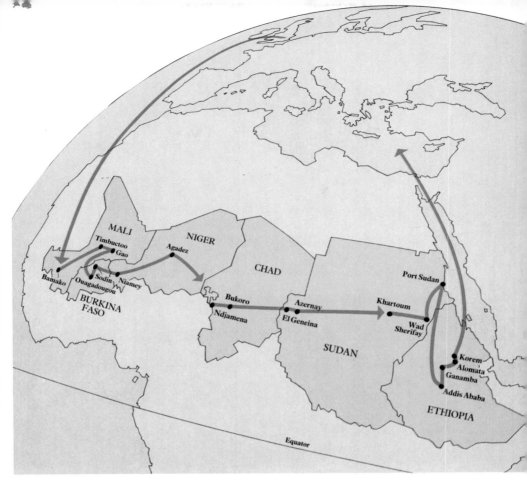

the problem was not just hunger, disease, or displaced farmers. It was more fundamental. The feeding camps were only staving off the real problem. Money was being spent on the wrong things. People were being used.

He was taken to meet someone who had been involved with death, disease, and poverty far longer than he — a tiny, wizened woman in worn-out sandals — Mother Teresa of Calcutta. Very small, very determined. In front of the television cameras, she asked a director of the Ethiopian Relief Commission if she could use as orphanages a couple of old palaces she had seen.

"I'm sure we can find you some suitable premises for an orphanage."

In October 1985, Bob Geldof made a journey across six of the African countries worst affected by drought and famine. He spoke to governments, aid workers, and hungry people. Bob studied aid projects and discussed how Band Aid donations should best be spent. He called it, "a trip to focus my outrage."

25

"Two orphanages," she prompted.

"Two orphanages," he agreed weakly.

Bob stared at her in awe. Here was a woman who could get things done. But not as Bob did. No, her plan was to work more quietly with the suffering. She held his hand as they parted and said, "Remember this. I can do something you can't do and you can do something I can't do. But we both have to do it."

Everything he saw horrified him. It was far, far worse than the news cameras had led him to believe. They couldn't show the heat, the flies, the stench, and the disease.

One child summed it all up. He was about two, but with the body of a four-month-old baby, his eyes caked with dust and flies, his only covering a piece of rag. He had eaten dry grain, and it had torn his insides to shreds. Life was draining away in diarrhea and pain, and he was crying. He stood no chance of survival. He was the same age as Bob's own little girl, safe and happy, warm and fed, back in England.

Bob went to see the important people. Officials, whether from government or relief agencies, were having to tread carefully here. They were dealing with a foreign government. They had to choose their words. Bob did not.

One official began a polite, well-rehearsed speech. Geldof interrupted him and told him to stop talking nonsense, to come to the point, and to be honest about what needed to be done, what help was wanted and what cooperation his government could offer. The man tried to dodge the questions, but Bob Geldof is very good at refusing to let anyone dodge *anything*. He banged the table.

Leaving a flabbergasted set of politicians behind him, he went to the Sudan where he was told by officials that everything was totally under control. Tens of thousands were dying in camps without food, water, or sanitary facilities, but the officials said it was all under control.

At Tukalabab, he found a camp with no shelter except rags of cloth spread over the bushes and two

Opposite: Early in 1985, Europe spent $375 million destroying two million tons of surplus food. Even though he was busy organizing Live Aid, Bob Geldof felt so passionately about starving children like the one in the photograph that he talked to as many aid workers, politicians, and local experts as he could. He badgered them to see to it that Band Aid food and money were correctly allocated.

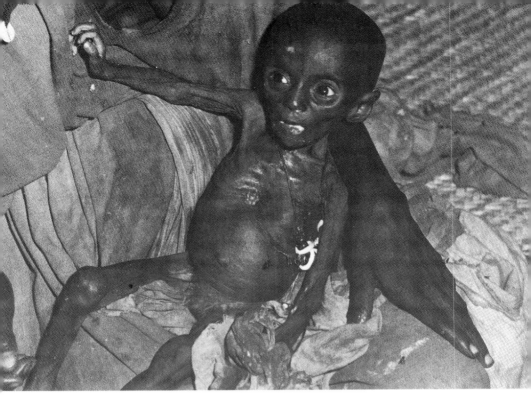

107946

27

Opposite: Bob, taking a break on his rushed trip through Africa. Everywhere he went, he drew crowds and he didn't always enjoy that. He called it the "Prince Charles Syndrome."

"I can do something you can't do and you can do something I can't do, but we both have to do it."
Mother Teresa
to Bob Geldof

doctors working in despair. The sun scorched the earth by day, and the nights were freezing cold. *The camp store had fifteen bags of flour to feed twenty-seven thousand people.*

Bob could see that millions more would soon be starving in the Sudan, yet the Band Aid record had been pledged to help only Ethiopia. More would have to be done. Much, much more.

Back in London, he tried to take up his career again but was deluged by requests to give speeches and to appear on television talk shows.

In the States, in January 1985, American pop stars were making their own aid record far more professionally than the British musicians had — the sleeker, slicker, shinier Hollywood way. Bob was asked to join them and flew over to record "We are the World." He was greeted with enthusiasm. It seemed a long, long way from his school days and Blackrock College. These people had been his idols

then and they still were. Now they too were working for Africa.

When the British record had been made, there had been one man guarding the door, and coffee and sandwiches from the local café if anyone got hungry. In the States, there was a massive show-biz party, with security guards everywhere, hangers-on eating smoked salmon and caviar, bottles by the score, diamonds, exhibitionism. Bob escaped to the studio to find reality — musicians doing a job and for free. Bob Dylan, Michael Jackson, Diana Ross, Paul Simon, Dionne Warwick, Stevie Wonder, Tina Turner, Ray Charles, Bruce Springsteen.

In spite of the glitz, the extravagance, and the showing-off by nonentities, the performers themselves were doing it all for free and for the same reasons as the musicians in London.

An idea began to grow in Bob's head. Band Aid? The British and American versions. Why not a concert? A big concert. The biggest concert ever. Britain and America — the whole *world* — working together for Africa.

Live Aid.

The idea is born

When the *USA for Africa* recording was over, Bob Geldof made a speech. He asked the American pop groups to join him if he was able to put together a concert for Africa. The idea was already taking shape in his mind.

He told the stars that finally the Band Aid record had raised $15 million, which seems a tremendous sum, but that it was only enough to keep those twenty-two million starving people alive for two weeks. It just wasn't enough. Something on a far larger scale was needed.

All around the world records like "Do They Know It's Christmas?" and "We are the World" were being made to help raise money for Africa — in France, Austria, Germany — twenty-five countries in all. But in show business, he knew only too well how quickly people's interest and enthusiasm fade. He knew that he must follow up the records with something really spectacular and as soon as possible — a pop concert, bigger and better than anything the world had ever seen. A single concert, linking America and Britain. The world.

He began to make notes and to talk to his friends about his ideas. "Great!" "Fantastic!" they said. But they thought he was absolutely crazy even to think of embarking on such a vast, unmanageable enterprise. They probably thought that once he realized what was involved, he would become discouraged and give up the whole crazy idea. They should have known better.

Since no one seemed inclined to help, Bob fell back to that old belief, "If you want to get something done, do it yourself." By March, Bob was moving forward. He set a date — July 13, 1985.

How would *you* begin? Think about it. Bands scattered on tour all over the world, with managers often demanding a percentage of the money. A date that would suit them all. Stadiums in America, Britain, West Germany, Holland, France, Japan, all large enough to accommodate performers, press and audiences. Television and radio coverage. The press. Transportation for the musicians. Catering. Advertisements. Souvenirs to bring in more cash. Telephones to accept donation pledges. The mind-boggling transmission technicalities. The problem of global differences in time. Satellite link-ups across the entire face of the earth. Where would you start? Especially if you had no money?

Live Aid — Making it work

Bob phoned Wembley, London's largest concert site. The secretary sounded hopeful. That was enough for Bob. He recruited Harvey Goldsmith, the promoter, and began the old round of calling every group he could think of who might draw a massive audience. This time the response was more overwhelming than it was with Band Aid. Even Bob Geldof was stunned. Top bands were offering to cancel concerts, to fly

"While . . . the intellectuals were debating the finer points of global politics and the problems that lay ahead when the charity ran out, Geldof was on the phone twenty hours a day organizing how best and how quickest the next life could be saved."
Barry McIlheney, Melody Maker, *Dec. 21, 1985.*

back from anywhere in the world just to be there. And of course they were asking no fee.

The phone calls grew more expensive — Australia, America, Spain, Canada, Japan, Italy — tracking down bands and getting their O.K.

He blithely asked the BBC for seventeen hours of non-stop use of television time. It seemed to him a very reasonable request.

Channel 4 television said they couldn't just cancel an entire day's transmissions, not for one concert. It would cost them over a million dollars. Bob blinked. He had not thought about that.

He phoned the States and recruited Bill Graham to promote that end. His ideas were met with a mixture of enthusiasm — and panic.

The number of performers was growing, but they had still heard nothing definite from London's Wembley Stadium. Wembley wanted a rental fee of about $200 thousand, reduced from over a million dollars, but still too much for Bob. Finding an American stadium was also causing problems. Finally, they got Philadelphia.

Australia wanted to come in on the link. Fine, but more technical problems.

And time was running out for the starving in Ethopia. Even Bob was getting nervous. But the concert was on its way.

Status Quo suggested they regroup, just for this one event. Bob's jaw dropped — cooperation! U2 agreed to come. Then Mick Jagger.

Bob seemed to be everywhere at once. He had to be. Everyone involved — and the numbers were growing with every day that passed — was working at top speed.

But it was Bob's trait of never taking no for an answer, of always going straight to the top, that did the trick. He phoned the airlines and organized them to ferry performers in. Free of course. He tackled the European Broadcasting Union. He wheedled and he bullied them.

It really did seem to be coming together. Even the trustees began to believe it would happen.

Russia wanted to take the concert, but only if the Americans were to give it top priority.

And America was proving to be a monumental problem. The Live Aid promoter there was going crazy with the negotiations, the promises, the letdowns, the demands, the refusals.

Some U.S. bands were being difficult and so were their managers. They didn't want to cancel bookings and commit their performers to a concert they weren't sure was really going to happen.

Some performers wanted to be treated as super big stars. Some worried about their image. Some worried about money.

Some were totally generous but not enough for this giant concert.

Meanwhile, in Britain, policing was no problem. Bob had phoned the Commissioner of Metropolitan Police and asked for it to be free. Yes, it would be. Over $15 thousand saved.

A catering company said they would donate ten percent of their takings if they were granted special privileges. Bob was very rude indeed. He told them that if they didn't give Live Aid all their profits, he would tell all the ticket holders to bring sandwiches and boycott the stalls and vendors.

British Telecom offered twenty phones to take the donation pledges. "I want *thousands*," said Bob. They didn't think it could be done in time.

So much to do, so little time. But in spite of all the bands with inflated egos, the managers with greedy pockets, and the television stations demanding to show only the very biggest names, things in the States were looking more hopeful every day. Some bands were knocking themselves out, working around the clock without asking a penny in return, paying for rehearsals, air fares, cancelling prestigious concerts, just to be at the Philadelphia concert. Bill Graham began to push other U.S. groups hard, trying to get across what it all meant. Some realized they would be in an embarrassing situation if they were known to have refused. More and more simply woke up to the urgency of Africa's need.

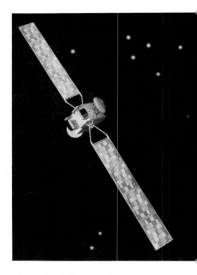

The television packaging was masterminded by the company that organized the Los Angeles Olympics. Sixteen satellites were arranged to beam the concert everywhere in the world.

Paula Yates, well-known television personality, backed Bob — financially and emotionally — during the time he worked for Live Aid. Bob and Paula have been together since 1977 and were married in July 1986.

The names were coming in. Madonna. Joan Baez. Judas Priest. The list was lengthening. But there were shocks, too. Bob was sure that the newspaper *Black Voice* would give enormous support to anything that would help Africa, the homeland from which the first slaves were snatched. Instead, they declared that Live Aid was racist and that there weren't enough black bands.

Bob couldn't believe it. David Bailey, the famous photographer, had paid all his own expenses to go out to Africa and photograph conditions, to draw the attention of the world to the suffering. *Black Voice* condemned him for spending money that should have gone to the poor. It seemed crazy.

President Ronald Reagan said he would send a message if Britain's Prime Minister, Margaret Thatcher, would too. Thatcher would not. There were plenty of other setbacks! Danish television wouldn't join in — they had always supported Lutheran Aid. French television, deciding "Pop music is not French," dismissed the whole idea.

Mike Mitchell, who was trying to get the American network tangle sorted out, was on the verge of total exhaustion. He had worked impossibly hard, and now the American Broadcasting Company (ABC) was making totally unacceptable demands. It really looked as if the whole thing could collapse.

The Germans said they couldn't give any money because it wasn't a German organization.

The Malayan television people asked if, please, they could keep what they raised? "Of course," said Bob. They were a poor country themselves.

It seemed *impossible* that it could get untangled in time. Geldof shuttled from Paris to New York to London. To Newcastle, Philadelphia, and back to New York. Then London again. He was dizzy, exhausted, and desperately worried. He was meeting incredible support and incredible stubbornness.

The Canadian Broadcasting Corporation (CBC) in Canada came up with a video, a short sequence showing a starving child trying desperately to get to its feet, courageous beyond all belief. They had edited it over The Cars' "Drive." It said everything Bob wanted to, and he told them that he wanted it to be shown at the concert.

Better and better. The Prince and Princess of Wales said they'd come. Royal approval.

Bruce Springsteen was due to appear at the Philadelphia end. He just couldn't make it. It was a bad disappointment, but Springsteen said he'd pay

"Almost everyone agrees that Geldof can be loud and obnoxious, has little politeness or tact, that he constantly uses language that isn't fit for a family newspaper, that he rubs people the wrong way, that he has no patience. Yet this man inspires the kind of trust that even the most respected charities can only dream of. People who would normally pass on by any hitchhiker, who looked like Bob does . . . walk up to Geldof with tears in their eyes and stuff wads of money into his hands."

Nathan Aaseng in his biography, Bob Geldof

for Wembley Stadium!

Bob's back was giving him terrible trouble. Too much travel, too little sleep.

Before he knew it, it was July 12. The concert was tomorrow.

Live Aid

July 13, 1985, was a beautiful morning. *More than eighty-five percent of the world's television sets, including those in the Soviet Union, would be switched on for Live Aid.* Two billion people would be watching. It was to be the biggest concert the world had ever known. According to *Time Magazine*, the twin concerts cost about $4 million and that was without the free services and all the

bands playing free. About $7 million from broadcasting and television rights. The day was already a mammoth fund-raising success even before the first song was sung.

But the man who had started it all, who had cajoled and bullied and planned and worked for this day, had agonizing back pain. He had lain awake into the small hours, his mind going over and over the thousand things that could go wrong. Now he was on his way to Wembley.

The crowds were already streaming into the arena. Those who spotted him arriving called out to wish him good luck. The doubts of the night were vanishing in the mounting anticipation. Even before the first note of music, there was excitement in the air, a feeling that everyone was in this thing together.

Backstage everything seemed chaotic. Bob told himself that this was just an illusion, that everyone knew exactly what they were doing. At least he hoped so. Some of the crew hadn't slept for two days, there had been so much to do and so little time to get it finished.

Out front the stadium was packed. Paula and two-year-old Fifi were there, and Bob's dad, pleased and proud and excited.

The Prince and Princess of Wales arrived. Fifi had been promised a smoked salmon sandwich if she presented Princess Diana with a bouquet. Handing over the flowers, Fifi remarked, "More fish please."

Bob Geldof — the bane of Blackrock College, the road builder, the slaughterhouse hand, the newspaper columnist, the lead singer of Nightlife Thugs — went up the little stairway into the royal box with Charles and Diana, up into the roar of enthusiasm that seemed to fill the entire sky. Even Charles and Diana seemed stunned by the sheer volume of that greeting. It didn't feel like a concert. It felt like a huge gathering of friends.

"God Save the Queen" gave way to "Rocking All Over the World." The concert had begun.

All the months of work, of sleepless nights, of arguments, negotiations and disappointments were over. This was it — the reality no one had thought possible. The huge audience rose to the music. Status Quo and Style Council had each done their stint. Now it was time for the Boomtown Rats. Bob worked his way through that vast audience to the stage. The music began, and it seemed that his back pain vanished as he launched into "I Don't Like Mondays." After it, he spoke to the crowd. It seemed to stretch out forever.

He said, "I think this is the best day of my life." Fifi was having a wonderful time. She was singing into Prince Charles' ear.

The Boomtown Rats were off and the next performer was on. Adam Ant. Everyone had the same time on stage. Not one act overran. No one

Elton John

The London finale: "I look around and tears are pouring down this collection of men and women. Sounds corny, doesn't it ... it wasn't."
Bob Geldof

David Bowie and Paul McCartney singing in the London finale. Bowie had decided to drop one of his songs for a video of Ethiopia. More money came in during these minutes than at any other time during the day. When Paul sang "Let It Be," the sound system failed. The crowd sang it for him instead.

39

The 80,000 crowd at London's Wembley Stadium.

tried to hog one minute of extra television time. Every act was allocated a dressing room, and every act had to get out of it at the time written on the pinned-up schedule. No one quibbled. This was no day for fits of star temperament.

Bob had no time to wind down from his performance. There was too much to do.

He watched the first television test of the coverage coming in from America and was horrified to see the cameras focus on scantily-dressed girls swaying on the shoulders of their boyfriends. He picked up the phone. This, he said, is in aid of the starving. It is worldwide. Plenty of countries on the link-up are a good deal more sensitive about this sort of thing than we are and could withdraw because of it. The cameras moved away to more conservatively dressed fans.

He phoned Ireland, wanting to know how his own country was doing. Money was already flooding in. Excited, he rushed to the donations' office, and discovered that Britain was well behind his country,

even though Ireland had only a twentieth of the population. It seemed insane. This was an appeal, not just a spectacular show. Where was the money? If the money didn't come, this would all be a huge, devastating failure, no matter how much everyone enjoyed themselves.

And everyone was enjoying themselves. INXS, far away in Melbourne, Australia, did their piece. Ultravox, Loudness from Japan, Spandau Ballet.

Two hours gone. America was under way with Bernard Watson and Joan Baez. Perhaps a slightly different style concert — more show biz, more speeches. But the audience was equally excited, and the money for Africa was coming in fast.

One after another, from all around the globe, the big and not-so-big names appeared. They were all eager to take part. They were all eager to raise money to help the starving.

Elvis Costello, then in the States, the Hooters. Vienna came in with Opus. Next Nick Kershaw, then the Four Tops. From The Hague, Holland — B. B. King, Billy Ocean, Run DMC. Belgrade with Yu

About 100,000 people in JFK, Philadelphia, and 1.5 billion people around the world.

41

Rock Mission.

At Wembley, Sade.

In Philadelphia, Rick Springfield.

And then, in London, Phil Collins, who was to make one of the major contributions of the day. The moment he had finished his performance, he scurried to a helicopter, was whisked to London's Heathrow airport, transferred to a Concorde and was off to Philadelphia. The Concorde was re-routed to fly low over Wembley; the crowd cheered them on their way.

REO Speedwagon, Howard Jones — then, from Moscow, Autograph. A real breakthrough.

Bob Geldof was here, there, and everywhere. No time to listen, only to watch the figures.

Brian Ferry. Crosby, Stills and Nash, who'd reunited for the first time in eight years. Cologne, Germany, with Udo Lindenberg. (Germany had agreed after all!) The links were working.

Judas Priest, Paul Young, Alison Moyet. And at five o'clock, Wembley time, Bob Geldof welcomed America. With so much that could have gone wrong, here they were on time, to the minute.

But everyone was having *too* good a time. Where was the money? It was coming in, but not enough, nowhere near enough.

Ireland, now Bob's touchstone, had topped one million. Women were pulling off their wedding rings and handing them in to save the children of Africa. But the British were still lagging far behind, and Bob was becoming frantic. He thundered through to the studio, ignoring the plan of presentation. To hell with presentation. There were people dying. He reached out to the huge listening public and urged them to call. Writing would take too long. They must get to their phones immediately. He said, "Listen, there are telephones here just lying dead. If you've sent your money already, go and bang on the house next door — and tell *them* to send some."

The British viewers, startled out of their procrastination, began to ring in.

He had hoped for a million dollars. By the end of the day, he had over $4 million. By the end of the

Live Aid was the most complicated telecast ever. Donations came in at the rate of 190 thousand telephone calls per hour.

week, over $30 million.

The music brought in the money, as Bob had believed it would. But as he had predicted, it was the CBC video that really woke up the nation. It was the video that hammered home the reason for all this effort, all this excitement.

That solitary child, struggling to get to its feet, starving and desperate but undefeated, said more than any lyric and any band, however famous, could say. This was Live Aid. This was what it was all about. And the money poured in.

The response from Ireland was still overwhelming. In the end it had donated more per capita than any other country — many far, far wealthier. But all over the world there were unbelievable acts of generosity, including one donation of a over a million dollars. The donations were mounting.

It was a wonderful afternoon. Wembley rose to U2 and Dire Straits. The sun shone and Queen performed brilliantly. The video "Dancing in the Streets" flashed onto the big screens and the magic of Mick Jagger and David Bowie bewitched the world. Later, Bowie himself came out to thunderous applause. "Let's do it again — *every* year!"

The Who appeared before an audience of millions, reunited after six years — Africa outweighed any personal problems. Elton John. Kiki Dee, Wham!

America kept pace. Bryan Adams. The Beach Boys, apparently ageless. George Thorogood. Bo Diddley. Albert Collins. The Pretenders. Santana and Pat Metheny. Ashford and Simpson with Teddy Pendergrass.

Teddy Pendergrass deserved his ovation more than anyone. There had been splendid, memorable moments, and this was one of the greatest. He was making his first appearance since an accident had left him paralyzed and in a wheelchair three years before. No talk of racism from Mr. Pendergrass. He just wanted to help the children living under the threat of starvation and disease.

There was Madonna in Philadelphia. Mercury and May came on in Wembley.

Aid for Africa concert at the Entertainment Centre, Australia. The Australians raised nearly $4 million for Band Aid.

43

Mick Jagger and Tina Turner

Lionel Ritchie

Ashford and Simpson with Teddy Pendergrass. Teddy is making his first public appearance — in a wheelchair — since an accident that left him paralyzed three years before. His voice grows stronger and stronger. Tears stream down his face as an almighty roar from the crowd drowns him out.

Opposite top: Patti LaBelle

Left: Madonna

45

And now Paul McCartney. To Bob it seemed a dream. To him the Beatles had been people apart, and now here was McCartney singing because he, too, cared about the children and because he, Geldof, had asked him to.

The British concert was coming to an end, and Bob realized suddenly that in all the confusion and haste, they had never rehearsed a finale. Hastily he handed out copies of "Do They Know It's Christmas?" and the motley collection of famous performers crowded around him backstage.

Some of the biggest names in the pop world fumbled through an impromptu rehearsal in the dark, because the power had failed.

On stage McCartney, who had been living for this moment, launched into "Let It Be." The microphone was dead. The audience did not care. They sang it for him.

By now, Bob's back was hurting so badly that he could scarcely stand. He stretched out backstage, just for a couple of minutes. And went to sleep.

The next thing he knew, he was being shaken awake and trundled onto the stage. Moyet, McCartney, Bowie, Townsend — and Geldof. As he stood there, he felt he had not awakened. The heroes of his lifetime and the boy from Blackrock standing together before that vast, happy, cheering audience.

After ten hours of thrilling pop music, it was a finale to end all finales. Everyone crowded onto the stage behind them, many with tears pouring down their faces. It wasn't show biz. It was a bunch of tired but happy people singing together — unrehearsed and from the heart. It had been a day without regrets — no sulks, no tantrums, no rivalry. A day to remember.

The British end of the great concert was over. The Wembley crowds slowly ebbed away, leaving the great arena scattered with litter and memories.

Backstage, there was an atmosphere of exhaustion and euphoria. They had finished one minute over time — which wasn't, come to think of it, bad at all!

Bob couldn't ignore the pain in his back any

longer. A doctor gave him an injection to ease it a little. He and Paula headed for the car that was to take them back to London, where they were to watch the last third of the American concert. There was no car to be seen.

It was not an evening to worry. They simply got a lift from a couple they met outside. The people they passed in the streets recognized them and called out, as if to old friends. Just for once, everyone seemed to agree about something, to feel they had all shared in something worthwhile, something worth doing.

The whole world had sung together — Japan, Finland, Russia, Austria, Yugoslavia, Britain, Norway, Holland, Australia, America. Even the Germans, who had seemed dead set against it all, had done an outstanding job.

Philadelphia was still awake and singing when Bob and Paula at last reached the night club where the Wembley performers were seeing Live Aid out to its very end.

In the States, Tom Petty, Kenny Loggins, The Cars, Neil Young, The Power Station, The Thompson Twins, and Eric Clapton had done their outstanding best, and now came Phil Collins, seemingly unaffected by jet lag but slightly amazed that he had actually arrived!

He had probably had the most extraordinary day of all, playing on both sides of the Atlantic in the same concert.

At Philadelphia, there was a different atmosphere backstage. In London, there had been scarcely any security and the whole thing had seemed more casual. Philadelphia policed more carefully. But it didn't matter. Phil Collins sang and it was still the same concert, though an ocean away from home. The difference in place did not affect the enthusiasm of the audience or stop the money from rolling in.

Plant, Page and Jones. Duran Duran. Patti La Belle. Hall and Oates (who'd given up a $125 thousand engagement to be there)! Eddie Kendricks, David Ruffin, Mick Jagger with the remarkable Tina Turner. Bob Dylan, Keith Richard, Ron Wood. And

"I have been blessed in my life and I don't take my good fortune for granted. That's what Live Aid is all about."
Patti LaBelle

"We will move a little from the comfort of our lives to understand their hurt."
Joan Baez

47

then, at 11:00 P.M. in the States and 4:00 A.M. in Britain, it really *was* the end, the end of the most incredible, memorable day in the history of pop music. One of the most remarkable days in the history of the world.

Bob Dylan was supposed to wind up the Philadelphia concert, but someone with a touch of genius got Lionel Ritchie back onto the stage to sing the American song for Africa, "We are the World."

Dawn was breaking as Bob Geldof and Paula finally went home to bed. It had been a good day. One of the best.

The donations roll in

By December 31, 1985, $92 million had reached the Band Aid offices. It was not over, though. The money was still pouring in, in fantastic amounts, and now it had to be organized for effective use. In a way, the really hard work lay ahead.

Bob still couldn't turn back into a Boomtown Rat, even though he longed to. The money had to be put into the hands of the best, most competent, and knowledgeable experts he could find. And the food and tools, the clothing and medical aid had to be

"If there is a meanness, an empty cynicism, a terrifying selfishness . . . in us, then that day, watching that television, dancing in that crowd, playing on that stage, the obverse side of our cruelty was made manifest. In an almost preposterous display of bravura, the world linked itself tangibly. . . ."
            Bob Geldof

directed to the people who needed it. Euphoria could not do that, only hard work and weeks of negotiation and effort.

To have been in the stadium was to have been with friends. And even those who could only watch at home had felt some of that sharing, had felt a part of it, too. An unforgettable atmosphere had pervaded the entire day and changed the world a little.

And now, no one could say they didn't know what was happening in Africa.

After the party

Band Aid was over. The Live Aid concerts were over. In the time it had taken to put them together, Bob Geldof had learned a great deal, not only about generosity, but about the real causes of the African disaster. He was becoming bitterly angry.

Bob Geldof was disturbed to find that he had become a hero. He didn't *feel* like a hero. All he felt he had done was to harness the good will generated by the situation in Africa to get together enough money to keep people alive until real solutions could be found. He had no illusions. He knew how big the problems really were, and he knew how quickly people would forget. But he had done more than raise money. He had given people a voice. He had been doing and saying things that ordinary people without power and influence had desperately wanted to do and say themselves. He seemed to speak for them, as their envoy. It did not take a high school diploma to realize that many of those in power were behaving with utter idiocy. Bob and his supporters knew it, and he said so, very loudly and clearly.

Live Aid and Bob Geldof bobbing up at important meetings all over the world could not alter national policies, but they *did* give those policies a nudge in the right direction. Governments don't like to look greedy, selfish, or foolish.

He was stunned to find himself in a position to influence governments, and being Bob, he decided to make the best use of the opportunity. He did not ask for miracles, only that they take a good hard look at their policies and that they give sane, practical, basic help and advice to those who needed it. He wanted them to put the suffering people first.

The West had been very generous. It had poured millions and millions of pounds and dollars into aid in the years before the Ethiopian tragedy. But sometimes the money had been given with selfish motives — for political reasons or to help the West's own markets. Some money had been spent unwisely on "prestige" projects or without consulting the people who best understood the land and what was needed. Often aid had made things far worse.

The West had made terrible mistakes. Its actions were based on what they knew about Western agriculture, Western economics, Western lifestyle. For example, eighty percent of the food in Africa is grown by women, but the "experts" from the West had given less than two percent of the aid to projects organized by women. This upset the whole balance of life in the countries where these women lived.

Governments had also introduced damaging changes. Nomads had been taxed and had been forced to settle to earn cash. Land had been reorganized. Yet making nomads live in one place upset the centuries-old system of grazing and helped turn pasture into desert. No one listened to them or understood their wisdom.

The West saw how expensive fertilizers and farming equipment and irrigation had increased their own crops and made fewer and fewer people necessary to work the land. They did not consider that the poorer countries couldn't afford equipment, fuel, or repairs. But by using both the simple tools they could make and the many, many people available to work, those countries could improve their way of life beyond belief, simply with sound advice and a little help.

Aid to Africa

Bob Geldof saw for himself how wealthy nations had flown in food at enormous expense, when building a road would have cost no more and would have served

"If he had been a more sophisticated man, more conscious of the difficulties of political initiative in a complex world, Geldof might never have broken through the bureaucracies which too often ensnare international relief. But his impulsive candour, exuberance and Irish charm saw him win every argument."

Geoffrey Wansell in The Sunday Telegraph

> *"We could spend our money tomorrow, and it could keep thirty million people alive for seven weeks, and then they'd die. Or, we can build wells and give them a life. I prefer to do that."*
> Bob Geldof

the people for generations to come. He saw great, white, clean hospitals in the cities and no medical aid at all out in the countryside. He saw the mismanagement, the muddle, the rivalries between government departments and even aid societies. He saw the damage that ignorance and selfishness can do to powerless people.

He knew he was no expert, so he spoke to the experts. After the concert, he went and saw for himself. He asked questions. He cornered important people who tried to flatter him and put him off with smiles and glib answers. He forced them to talk about the truth of the matter — what had been done, what needed to be done.

Bob Geldof had learned quickly. His intelligence, honesty, and sheer common sense cut through all the polite excuses and phony explanations. He wanted answers. Fast.

He found it strange to be speaking as an equal to Tip O'Neill and Teddy Kennedy in America, to African leaders, to the Ethiopian Parliament. But he had long since learned to put aside names and titles

and to see influential people as individual human beings. To him, Prince Charles was not just the future King of England, but a kind, intelligent, caring man, a man he liked and trusted. Other leaders he viewed with a more jaundiced eye.

Back to Africa

Bob unnerved people with his direct approach, but he won great respect and got answers.

The Press, to his surprise, ignored the vindictive gossip about him. They knew him and they liked him. He swore and he roared when roaring was needed, but he was absolutely honest. They said he must go on, that he must go back to Africa.

He felt inadequate to take on such a task, but he knew he must go. He could not leave a job half finished even if, by this time, his own finances were in a terrible mess. Mercifully, Paula was doing well in her jobs as writer and television personality. She took it on herself to keep things afloat at home. After

Band Aid purchased over two hundred trucks to ensure that the food actually got through to the starving people in remote areas. Three Band Aid ships sailed every week from London to Africa, carrying more trucks, jeeps, tents, and medical aid and supplies of grain, flour, and vegetable oil.

Bob receives the United Nations Food and Agriculture medal for his Band Aid and Live Aid work. Bob, Irish-born, is handed the award in Dublin by the Irish Prime Minister, Dr. Garret Fitzgerald.

all, he and she were a team and a very good team at that. He would leave in October.

In Africa, Bob developed, of all things, an in-grown toenail. That sounds like a silly complaint — unless you have had one. It became badly infected and Bob was in great pain, but with the unfortunate toe swathed in bandages like a grubby turban, he limped through the Sudan.

He knew he had to push on. He knew only too well that the more he was able to see, the more issues he forced into the open, the more the ordinary people of the world would know of the truth, and of the necessity for action.

The European Parliament

Back from the Sudan, Bob went to Strasbourg to confront the European Parliament. It was explosive. He hadn't written a speech. He just let things rip that had been boiling in his mind for months. He attacked Europe's Common Agricultural Policy for a start, knowing the misuse of subsidies that went on.

He talked about Chad and the involvement of the French. The French representative got to his feet and shouted. Bob shouted back. The French man stomped out.

To Bob's amazement, everyone seemed to be on his side. Everyone was applauding practically everything he said. He was saying what many people wanted to say, but dared not.

"The worst thing is that a lot of what the European Economic Community does is excellent," he said. "You are the second biggest donor in the world. The airlift you have organized to the west of the Sudan has been an incalculable success. There's no disputing that. But the stupidity is that if you'd listened to the warnings you were given in the first place, you could have built a road for what that airlift cost. And a road would have been there next year."

He found all the facts and figures that he had pored over for months suddenly there in his head. He could bring evidence for every accusation, statistics to back up every demand.

He could scarcely believe he had done it. He could scarcely understand the applause. He felt he hadn't done anything worthwhile. There was so much to do, and he felt totally inadequate. But he had made some impact.

Bob went to Australia. He knew what he wanted from them and asked for it — 250 thousand more tons of grain for Africa, help in establishing research stations based on the unique knowledge Australia gathered from its own barren-land agriculture, the refurbishment of ten aged Hercules aircraft for use in emergencies. He didn't get everything he asked for, but he got something.

Bob, the Knight

They gave Bob Geldof a lot of awards, a lot of medals. On July 24, 1985, they even gave him a knighthood. Paula went with him to Buckingham Palace to receive it. She said he looked like a naughty boy at a prize giving, but she was proud of him. So was everyone. The *Belfast Telegraph* quoted Harry Greenway, a British Member of Parliament: "This is a high honour and a just one, to an outstanding Irish and world citizen. He inspired a whole generation."

Bob squirmed a little, but accepted everything on behalf of all those people behind the scenes whose names got no publicity — the Boomtown Rats, who'd risked all with him; the organizers of Band Aid; the pop stars; and above all Paula. He knew what they had done if no one else did.

By the end of 1985, Band Aid alone had raised over $10 million, Live Aid had raised $60 million, not only for Ethiopia, but also for the Sudan, Mali and Chad. Spinoff projects added to the sum. *USA for Africa* contributed more than $42 million. "We are the World," plus Sports Aid, Fashion Aid, and the other spinoffs from countries all over the world are estimated to be well over another $50 million.

This money had bought two hundred trucks, nine ships, and seventeen thousand tons of grain to save those on the edge of death. He had poked and pried

Bob Geldof and the head of Band Aid, Kevin Jendon, at a press conference in Addis Ababa. Between them is the deputy-head of the Ethiopian Government Relief and Rehabilitation Commission. The board behind them shows a breakdown of the world's donations to famine relief during the previous year.

Opposite: Ethiopia is heading for another famine in late 1987. The concern of Bob and all aid workers is to work ahead to prevent starvation in this and all future famines. But the outlook is not good.

and bullied and questioned, looking for ways to prevent it from happening again and again. Band Aid had made a start on those essential long-term projects. It had built schools and clinics, put up houses, and given people the chance to take up life again, to use their minds and skills, and to regain their human dignity.

According to *The Times* in London, "Money has been given to a women's cooperative in Mopti, Mali: a tree planting scheme in the Sahel: a brickmaking project in Timbuctoo: a bee-keeping enterprise in the Sudan. The priority, after the rehabilitation schemes, was returning people to the lives they lost in the famine by giving them oxen, seeds, and fertilizers. Money goes to low-key projects which take the needs and realities of local life into account."

The wave of human emotion that swept the world when it discovered the plight of Africa had lead to some important, lasting changes, but the real solutions still have to be worked for, year after year.

The wonderful golden glow of Live Aid is over.

At the University of Kent degree ceremony, Bob accepts an honorary MA degree. The awards keep coming for this scruffy, informal, blunt Irishman. All the important people can forget the swear words when a man has raised over $140 million for the poorest people in the world.

Euphoria is glorious, but it doesn't last long. The starving, the homeless, the terrified are still there. The destruction of our planet by the shortsighted goes on.

And things are actually getting worse. In a hard-hitting article, London's *Observer* newspaper stated the facts: "Per capita incomes are now lower than they were in 1970, and are expected to fall, even on the most optimistic assumptions, for the next decade. A fifth less food is produced for every African than in 1960. If this trend continues, the crop in 1988 will be no better than 1984's disastrous harvest, even if the rains are good. Much of this is the fault of African governments who have starved their farmers of resources and pursued wildly inappropriate economic policies. But just as much, if not more, has been beyond their control."

Bob Geldof was born white and Irish, but he grew up to be a citizen of the world. That doesn't mean to say he has a glazed look of love and peace on his face, as he makes uplifting speeches. He can be difficult, profane, loud, churlish.

"I seem rude and surly to a lot of people," Bob admitted to a *Daily Mail* reporter, "but I seemed that way at 18. I *am* dogmatic . . . always talking about things other people should do and I see things in terms of black and white." But some of the people he shocks need it. They have been hiding behind smiles and pleasantries so long that when the truth is pushed under their noses, it comes as a terrible surprise.

Of course he has made mistakes, gone too far, hurt some people who didn't deserve it. But fundamentally he is an honest man who, as he says himself, cannot stand hypocrisy. He will not allow things to slide for the sake of a comfortable life.

Diplomacy can often work as well or better than insult and anger, but there is always the danger that it can be just a little too smooth, too careful, too slow. Too nervous. Occasionally a Bob Geldof is needed, just to get things going. And the results can be spectacular!

The African Famine
— *background information*

One aid worker described one of the main feeding camps in the north of Ethiopia in late 1984 as "hell on earth." At that point, famine had spread right across sub-Saharan Africa from Mauritania in the west to Ethiopia in the east. Part of the cause was that a decrease in rainfall in the entire region caused crop failure. This had been going on for several years, so reserves of food diminished until there was nothing left.

But this was only part of the problem. The population of these countries was increasing, thanks to modern medicine. This increased population, needing wood for homes and fuel, cut down forests. Without forests, soil eroded. The end result was that the land deteriorated and was less able to produce food for these extra people. At the same time, the national debt and inflation rates in the ten or so countries involved were greatly increasing so that much of the money aid given by the West was eaten up just paying the interest on the debt. In Tanzania, for example, in 1972 it required thirty-eight metric tons of sisal to buy a seven-ton truck. In 1982, it required 134 tons.

In Ethiopia, Sudan, and Chad, civil wars have flared up on and off for several years. Add to that inadequate transportation systems, government policies that ignored the farmers, and misdirected aid, and you have a recipe for the disaster that occurred. As the Catholic Fund for Overseas Development report stated bluntly, "Like all disasters, famine selects its victims. It is the poor and vulnerable members of society that are most exposed. . . . Three-quarters of the victims . . . have been women and children."

Aid agencies and the government of Ethiopia had been saying that a famine was imminent for more than a year before the television report burst onto our screens and shocked Bob Geldof and the world into action. Unfortunately, the Ethiopians did not initially appear to be very concerned about it, and the message did not get through. They weren't the only ones. "We do not consider drought an emergency," said the European Economic Community (EEC) office in Addis Ababa in early 1984. "Only when people start dying of starvation does it become an emergency."

Once the world realized what was happening, aid started flooding in. But by that stage, more than thirty million were facing starvation and hundreds of thousands had left their homes in search of food. Some food aid had arrived through the Red Cross, aid agencies, and the EEC. But for many it did not arrive in time. Officials estimate that up to a million people died in Ethiopia as a result of the famine in 1984-1985.

Although the immediate crisis ended with a good rainy season in 1985, the long-term problems continue. In 1987, drought is forecast. Aid-givers have